Contested Terrain

¤

D. A. Gray

FUTURECYCLE PRESS
www.futurecycle.org

Library of Congress Control Number: 2017953603

Published by FutureCycle Press
Athens, Georgia, USA

ISBN 978-1-942371-38-0

For my wife, Gwendolyn. Thank you for everything.

*For all veterans, those who've returned and those still struggling to return.
You are never forgotten.*

*For the Hambidge Center for Arts and Sciences.
Thank you for offering such a special place in the mountains,
and peace of mind while working on these drafts.*

Contents

CAVE COUNTRY

DESERT SUN

RETURNING TO THE HILL COUNTRY

A HANDFUL OF DUST

CAVE COUNTRY

Cave Country

Consider the sinkhole formation, the sudden black dot
emerging from green pasture, growing, eating, swallowing.
Cool air spills from below, bends the scorched grass.

Consider the properties of this formation—the presence
of dark, the absence of light, moist ground beneath
the dry surface—a lost trust that the earth

will continue to hold. Consider how the world you know
is cut in two. As you descend, first the feet and then
the legs disappear, then the hips and then the head.

But, you protest, you are still present. The heart's evidence
taps against the temple, the way it does when tense.
Consider everything you know of burial,

of underworlds, all the stories of black and white.
Consider whether you've changed one damned bit,
not being seen but felt, sometimes heard.

Consider the meaning of darkness without
the mythologies of hell, that place where what
you thought was true, has started to shift.

Cincinnati

It is 1967, and Martin and Bobby, still alive,
    light a spark with their voices,
and in a Johannesburg hospital, Dr. Barnard
    has pulled the first beating heart
from a fading woman, stitched
    it into an open cavity and shocked
it into a rhythm it will hold for eighteen days,
    and the world begins to hope
for stays of terminal sentences,

    and in Vietnam, four hundred seventy-four
thousand sleep amid rice and manure.
    Boys firing into the darkness
find hasty prayers answered with orange halos.
    And back home, Ginsberg, Spock
and two hundred sixty long-haired freaks
    protest the draft, head to jail
from Whitehall Street if only for a night,

    while in Ashland, Kentucky, a man and woman
begin the drive toward Ohio,
    ten years married. December has seen
a gentle fog rise from the river basin
    up through the mountains,
obscuring evidence of life, the smoke pouring
    from scattered chimneys,
the smell of burnt hickory and salt-cured ham.

    The man has just been discharged,
but in his mind danger still lurks over each ridge
    as he drives in silence. The woman
wraps a shawl tighter against the cold.
    And Big Sandy flows into the Ohio,
mountains turn to hills, and wheels scrape
    across a frozen metal bridge.

Her foot taps to the percussion of road seams,
    taps to keep back the cold,
and steam rises from the river
    like ghosts.

The couple drives into Cincinnati
        where a teenaged mother cries—scared—
and I am delivered from a room
        I'll never see again, screaming a sound
still searching for the shape of words.

Bottle Feeding Time

Each spring the newborn steer arrived, being bought
and trucked from the dairy farm three miles away.
Freshly banded scrotums beginning their numb descent,
a smell of fresh-burned hair where the nubs of horns
once pushed through the skin. Like children, their legs
shook in a cool April morning; big, black eyes searched
for mother while I stood at the iron gate holding
her surrogate plastic teat. "Don't name them,"
was the only instruction I got—and ignored. I called
out to Jack each night at feeding time. Jack had learned
to poke a black and white face through the red gate,
wrestle for the bottle. And if I failed the proper angle
he'd run a pink sandpaper tongue and a gallon
of drool across my small, pale fingers.

By late winter something hardened. What cattle
remained dotted a distant hill, huddled against the cold.
We'd notice from the farmhouse window, or look
when the wind caught the iron gate and whipped
it to the limits of its chain.
                              And toward dinner time
one of us would fetch a pack of round or rib
from the basement freezer. It took some time,
the sorting through cold, stacked squares. Dry fingers
ached from flipping and searching for the right
block-lettered name stamped on butcher paper.

In rare moments I thought about those labels
at feeding time and, when there was talk,
began to address each person, speaking their names
slowly, carefully, feeling the air begin to warm
as those letters and syllables ran across my tongue.

Nocturne

Everything not anchored to the ground
begins to move. The tin roof, on one side,
pries itself loose from the chicken coop.

The wind won't quit its game of pulling
up the metal sheet and letting
it crash again. Wood-handled rakes
lift away from the toolshed before falling,
tapping out a quarter note pulse.

The plastic shroud above a bed
of tobacco plants has come unmoored;
one corner rises. Soon, it will lift and roll
end over end, wrap around a barbed

wire fence. Rusted points will leave
the sheet tattered; one loose end crackles.
Above farmhouse steps, a screen door opens,

strains against its hinges, and slams shut
to accompany the wind's alto whistle
that rises around the brick edges of a world

eerily absent of lyric,
                              the cattle having departed
deep into the woods, dogs curled upon themselves,
and us lying in the black, pretending to sleep.

Contested Terrain I

Colors of spring have turned upside down.
Red once burned underfoot, now hangs
over the horizon—a blood bruise where sky
smashed itself against hills. Green once gathered
in the quick-shaping clouds carrying a mix
of sand and rain and left quickly as it arrived;
now it cushions your steps, hides the evidence of bones.

Cadiz

There's nothing in this warm, vegetal dusk
That is not beautiful or that will last.
—Joe Bolton, "Tropical Courtyard"

At the end of Main Street, the sun pulls the road
a little lower each day before disappearing into green.
Six storefronts on each side become downward
heading stairs—that's the "rage against geometry."

And the road I'm driving, looking for some residue
or fingerprint that is yours, falls faster than the storefronts
where old-timers stare at drive-through traffic, whittle, spit,
speak in staccato. Maybe they've earned their seat of judgment,

having outlasted the rest, in the shade of a wooden awning.
The temperature rises.
                              Molecules hang in the air
and the light disperses. It is that time washed
in a dirty gold patina, when walking becomes akin to drowning.

I take my foot off the brake pedal I've been riding
since the city limit sign. Descent pulls my old Fury
faster toward the other side. A whitewashed steeple
marks the end of civilization, and across the street
a Texaco station sign hangs by its last unbroken finger.

Here, a momentary lapse into acclivity triggers
the thought that enough speed could lift a man
out of this town, flying, leave little care for what waits
beneath the camouflage of green maple leaves
or little care for what waits when the fact of flying ends.

Two for Robert Penn Warren

I. In Guthrie

Uphill from the sheet metal shack, rust drips
from twin sliding doors and the sliding track hangs
off-kilter; and uphill from a barely seen Purina checkerboard
that bleeds through whitewashed cinder blocks,

Mr. Warren's home has become museum of red-
painted brick. The wind rocks empty chairs on a wraparound porch;
a CLOSED sign peers through the glass-paned door.
A sound of great geese hovers in the air,

and the world passes downhill from an unread sign.
The words *Laureate* and *Pulitzer* fade into the corner
of Cherry and Third. A truck idles beside the marker.

The driver is looking for the American Café,
for blackberry cobbler, steaming joe, and the sound
of tall tales, a sound that hovers while, beneath it,
drivers do what drivers do in small-town Kentucky—

watch for signs and pass straight through.

II. Waking

Beneath a grey sky pressing down,
the growl of spinning blades. It is
lawnmower feeding time, the hunting
and gathering before the storm. Machine
is cutting stems off at their base,
leaving a green and coumarin wake.

The mower hums; the man behind follows.
The song they're moving to is "Hurry."
Life springs up faster than man
and machine can respond. It makes him
feel inadequate, and now the mower
has *murder* in its heart.
                    "Hurry,"
is the first song I hear. Already dawn,
the light has broken in past venetian blinds.

It's sitting on my bed and waiting
while the past—last night's dream, assembled
from a mishmash of years—
is slipping out of my hands. By the time
I can name the sound, the mower stops.

Rain has begun to drum on shingles;
the nearby road has picked up the tune
beneath a trucker's wheels, lunging,
racing without thought toward tomorrow.

Keeping Time

Winter nights the dark becomes an edge against grey
seeping light; the cold speaks and it is '77 once more.

Against an interior wall the grandfather clock,
each pendulum swing a turn of toothed gears,
keeps a backbeat while my father sweeps ashes
from the Franklin stove into a wrought iron bucket.

He crumples yesterday's news into the chamber,
covers it with splinters, twigs and frozen logs. He strikes
a single match and watches—soon, ice will pop,
shatter and scream its escape from between logs. Wind calls
from the chimney; voices echo atop the metal flue,
where heat gathers. Soon smoke from the center answers,
rising.
         In the next room, Mother stares in silence,
piercing needle and thread into canvas stretched by a metal hoop.
Her feet curl beneath her. Under the brass floor lamp
she sews a golden sun rising over a spring pond;
with white thread, the presence of light shimmers
off the blue surface. Her other hand pushes fabric taut;
fingers rise, pushing to the surface, like panicked fish.
Here the blue threads expand on the canvas.
The tranquil surface holds for now.
                              Father stares
into the furnace until satisfied the fire's glow will last a few
more hours, then closes an iron door with hands blackened
by all the ashes swept before.
                         Between rooms, the pendulum swings;
the counterweight drops—a brass teardrop, which is
only a teardrop when it's falling, never when it falls.

River Styx, Kentucky

At the confluence, the hawk and wood drake have ceased
their chatter; only creek babble rises from the black
spilling from a cave mouth that hangs, grief frozen
open like some Greek chorus mask. Sun burns through
a canopy of elm and sycamore branches, resting
on the eyelids like silver dollars.
                                        This is the place
where you told me warriors came to rest centuries ago,
mining for gypsum or healing their wounds.
Later, tourists followed sign stacked upon sign,
risked falling into an unseen hollow for an adventure
and a photograph. The breeze and the green glow
from the water, you said, were their souls still trying
to cross; you laughed when I shivered.
                                        You, still alive then,
told me once of days spent crossing by ferry and of the boatsman
who, though his glare seemed angry, had warm hands
and helped each passenger board. You remembered the way
he spoke of sounding the depths, of the way light blazed
from the tiny bodies of creatures, and of things unseen
beneath the green glow. You, just widowed, asked him of family.
In response, he looked to where the Styx spilled into the Green,
never said another word.
                                        Now, only moss remains,
cratered where the old landing sinks into the water
and in the wheel-formed ruts that climb up from the edge,
on the other bank, and disappear into the woods.

Driving Past the Jefferson Davis Monument

After a summer shower, the two-lane road
departing Highway 68 begins to steam.
The road snakes between grazing land, cornfields,
family cemeteries in a crazy-quilt design

bordered by black walnut and red oak trees. Seeds,
crushed to the earth, now thrive in fencerows,
where DeKalb and Monsanto signs hang;
a horse-drawn plow rusts in the weeds.

My feet once balanced on these metal frames
of abandoned tools. Gleaming silver blades
would cut fresh wounds in the soil where I rocked

back and forth, and a clevis shackle—useless
without labor and mules—sang its southern chime.
Beneath these blades, between the weeds,
the red clay seeped.
                                    In farmhouses like these,
rising from the roadsides, we took lunch with the hands,
listened to news of a newer oncoming war
that seemed like a video game on the television.
Someone would say freedom. It sounded honorable
dying for an abstraction.

                              The whirring brings me back.

A gunmetal grey Chinook passes over, flying west—
Ft. Campbell. The blades slice an unmoving air.

On the ground, a Mennonite couple drives
a black carriage pulled by a chestnut horse.
They, too, travel west from the Elkton stores.
The young man, with the beginnings of a beard,

grips the leather reins; the woman has worked
her arm through his. They wave smiling as if the world
will wait, before gliding past me. My windows down,
radio up, I read a map and wipe a bead of sweat.

Everything is too slow to provide relief
from a sun just begun to bear down.

And behind the carriage, a line of cars inches
forward in a slow, fruitless stampede. On-again-
off-again brake lights with warnings of red eyes
glare into the past. Everything hinges

on this carriage, this horse, beneath a tall
white obelisk rising above the trees, a monument
to lost causes, six hundred thousand gone—
no gallantry, only mud.

                    Inside the monument,
his picture hangs—he must have sat an hour,
glass catching the light, battle orders in front,
Stars and Bars behind, eyes focused on a theory
boys would die from. Another picture exists.
An older white-headed man sits alone, cross-
legged on a bench. Both images are the same.

From this roadside I can see the visitors walk
from their cars to its base. A red truck passes,
slows, begins to turn without a signal. On the tailgate
a bumper sticker colored with Stars and Bars
says *Freedom.* "Free from what?"
I ask, but my voice dies in the thick air.

It's getting late; the tower's shadow lengthens.
Somewhere Mennonite families extract the last labor
from the last daylight. Fort Campbell soldiers
stand saluting a flag they are willing to die for,
before driving home on Blue Star Memorial.

Here, cars resume their speed, slide
past a tower once designed to mark temple gates.
Purpose forgotten, it stands pointing skyward
where insubstantial clouds slither past.

Orange

"Say orange again," she needles me and my Pennyrile accent.
It is an old joke—"Orange ya glad"—something rhymes?

For years I practiced dropping that accent from the window
of a car speeding down some western highway but stopped
at the word orange, unable to form that mouth-pained O,
to birth the sound of fruit, of jack-o-lanterns and fire,
of farm work, soil and solitude
                       or to erase the residue of childhood.

The last light of our subdivision has begun to bleed
from gold to garnet and soon will turn to black, bringing trick-
or-treaters out. The smaller children already creep
up the street with parents in tow, and as we wait with fists
of Tootsie Rolls and Candy Corn, a shiver comes across my shoulders.

I wonder what occupies the youths in neighborhoods
who walk the street sides together with glad hands
waving to strangers.
                 Glad is a sky anything but orange—
and since we're waiting at the door, I tell a story about glad.
"While most kids carried pumpkin-shaped pails door to door
on a quest for sugar highs on the All Saints Eve of penance
and puking,
           I would cup my hands in the cold air,
warming them with hot breath, expecting the season's
first frost. My old man would reach into a cardboard box,
count out five shotgun shells, and drop them in my
makeshift basket."
             "You think your childhood was
so different?" my wife says, grinning. "Just last year police were
looking for the kids who broke windows on the corner house,
the one that's still unsold."
             She stops—a father and son
walk toward the door, the older man dressed
as the Count, the boy a superhero we've never seen.

We drop the treats into the boy's hands; they say "Thank you"
and walk away. I think about "different" and begin again.

I begin again, wondering if she sees the weathered
tobacco barns, a year's wages in the tiers,
or warm-lit streets beneath sodium vapor lamps.

"I can still hear the old man's voice—'Point it down,
and never point it toward the house, never at anyone
unless you're ready...'
                            and we ready by balancing
pumpkins from the patch on top of fence posts, firing
practice shots until we no longer see the gourds burst.

I learned not to believe in orange sunsets then,
the color of runaway fires set by Halloween pranksters,
but only in Remington, only in my back against
a weathered tinderbox barn.

                        October air dried and hardened the skin.
The old man never shivered, and so I learned to stand expressionless.
Tobacco dust from where the year's labor hung burned my nose.
We took turns on watch, waiting for a tragedy that never came."

She pushes the screen door open, looks across, then down.
The street's gone quiet, and the glow above the hillside
comes from a distant road.
                        "Well," she says.
"Here the chances are the pranksters are only kids.
Your money's in the bank. Windows and mailboxes
can be fixed."
                    With that she shuts the door, and the steel lock
slides into the catch. We both exhale; the tension leaves us
just seconds before a siren splits the air.

Tolling

My mother drinks her tea in silence, listening;
the brass bell's echo plucks the steel chord of air.
Father watches the weather from his easy chair—
volume masks the knell from the back room, lingering.

Some nights she pours a third and, out of habit,
carries the cup to the empty room before she halts.
A voice she hears will hover, *Why do you never talk?*
Other nights she locks the door, turns her back, quiet.

Brushes and easels, dusty travel books fill the den;
a future life waits and survivors stare, patient
to outlive the mad, rude old lady who insists
on shaking her brass bell from a dark room. The din
of the departed wakes the living, and apparent
bells tap memory's nerve to say, *I still exist.*

Circular Logic

At the end of the cul de sac, beyond the radius of a street-
light's honeyed glow, sits a house and, in the house,
images run circles in a sleeping man's brain.

In exactly one hour the long hand will have spun
full circle. The alarm will sound. He will stumble
toward the porcelain bowl, aiming poorly

at the small circle, in those moments before coffee rises
in vapor from a round ceramic cup. But now those spheres
of eyes are shut. The brain's playing movies against

concave bone—some fusion of yesterday, a fucked-
up childhood, and who knows what. There's a hand
turning a steering wheel before opening, before letting

the textured plastic disk slide, spinning across his palm
as the world rights itself. Always this sensation
of turning wheels, guts churning, contents pinned

centrifugally to his ribs. He's rolling across asphalt—
in this recurring dream he's never aware of a destination.
Beneath a blood-red moon, our dreamer watches

the mishmash of images trapped in the diameter
of an eye. Later, the cylinder will hold a scene
of breakfast—beside a tiny round orange

will sit the morning paper, rolled and banded, waiting
for him to open it, to sit reading the classifieds,
pen resting in the loop he's made with thumb and forefinger,

waiting to circle an opportunity. The world bleeds
into the imagination. His mind begins to take hold
of the story, and suddenly there's the car again,

turning, turning, onto a familiar road.
He's headed home to the house at the end of the street,
under the extinguished light whose metal post

warms under a pale white disk. Hopes and failures
wait. Programmed coffee drips through the aperture,
rippling as it hits the surface. He pulls closer

to his wife's curved back. Soon the world will crash
through this geometry, but for a few more minutes he's content
to lift a knee, curling into an imperfect O.

Elegy for the Clockmaker

An anchor swings at the end of its escape
and, as it oscillates, each limit turns a set
of gears we only know from their clicking noise,
from the movement of black hands long and short.

Sometimes, through the casing's beveled glass,
I watch the pendulum swing and notice the line
where the angle changes, where the brass bob splits
itself in two.
               It's the back and forth that always
held my gaze, even after I'd moved away.

Six states, three countries, a lost accent—
and on each return I'd inspect the walnut case
we built—what, thirty now?—years ago.

My fingers would check for ridges across the grain
to feel what had risen from the past.

"When it feels like glass, you are done." I remember
your demanding voice, the jeweler's loupe hanging
from eyeglass. I laughed, even as a child,
at the sight of a watchful eye magnified beyond reason,

then resumed my work with the sanding block,
back and forth, always with the grain. And you'd return
to a workbench, metal parts stacked in labeled tubs,
a movement clamped to a pedestal, to resume

some adjustment of brass teeth, the tightening
of a metal spring, where a mistake of millimeters
could stretch seconds into hours or days.

Back and forth you'd venture, fingers checking
for rough spots in the wood, and when the surface
seemed smooth enough, you'd run a damp sponge
that lifted evidence of tree rings to start
the process anew.
                Now the clock ticks off
the minutes in my house, days ordered
by the clicks of teeth and springs. And you—
six years gone? My hand runs back and forth
across the case, and its blemishes,
which multiply with time, are mine.

Chicken Tree

Each autumn the air thins; the first chill strikes
sinuses like a sack of nails. Summer's last pear
has fallen, has lived as perfume, then rot,
and now has withdrawn into the tall weeds.

This is the time of year the sun rests on its darkening
leaves. It is the smell that draws me nearer: cut grass,
fruit rot, lilac, cow dung, and something I cannot name.
Returning home on the dry gravel road, I can see
a strange dirty-white fruit swaying from its branches.

Grandmother has grabbed the fattest chickens
from the henhouse, twisted the beaked end with her left,
swung a sharp hatchet with her right, and onto the ground
dropped the tiny heads. In the pause between the killing
and the eating, between life and the table, we gather to help,
tie feet to limbs, and leave the talons clutching at sky.

We smell the oncoming of winter and set water to boiling.
We prepare for the plucking, the cutting, the long freeze.
We work under bare branches, under a silent dripping
juice, under this tree where they've come home to roost.

Sugar Shack

Away from the tin roof, an old mare walks
circles around the cane press. Families feed
stalk after stalk through its teeth. Sugarcane
by the armload crushed, then carried beneath
the sugar shack roof. You watch with envy
this transformation, the gathering of the tribe.
Neighbors have come to celebrate the harvest,
as have you. One grocery item becomes
an all-day celebration. Steam rises from
the boiling pans, their treasure green and condensed.
You'd think God came down and condensed
the southern honeysuckle air, and she did.
It's not much different out from under the roof,
thick scent, a massive hand pressing down, you inside.

Lime

Our dog, a dachshund, was chewed to death
by a pack of domestics running loose at night.
And now I've said it. Time to get on with
the business of burial, be it carcass or memory.
We kept a bag of lime for such occasions.
On the farm, births happened without the sanitary
delivery rooms and death without the priest.
Because they happened imperfectly, we cherished
the ones that went right. It says something
when the means to cover the smell and speed the decay
lies within a short walk. We buried him
in the field above the tobacco patch where he'd wait
beneath the wagon for workers to emerge from the rows.
No marker, nothing sentimental.
He'd already begun to stink—that's how we found him—
decay being natural, as is the stupidity of domestic dogs
feeding their need to hunt and not knowing what to do
with their prey once they've ripped its throat.
So they run home to a friendly bowl of kibble,
and we're left to clean up their crime, which we do
enough in cave country. Even in passing the homes
of strangers, we recognize those dark mounds,
the bag of lime sometimes leaning, still, against the shed.

Shanty Hollow

It was never fair remembering only silence.

Surely words passed between father and son
on a pre-dawn drive where the skeletal shadows
of oak trees lurked above the sandstone cuts
that the road formed on its way out of town

or at the marina where hands pushed
a Styrofoam cup through moist dirt, feeling
for the fat bodies of night crawlers,
and where ears witnessed the sudden silence
of crickets as the door lifted and light entered.

So much in the silence was typical—
uneasy feet stepped slowly, finding the boat's center.
First the father, moving toward the outboard,
then the son, setting one by one the oars, vests,
stringers and tackle, rods and reels
between the seats.
                                    The outboard's growl
broke the calm. We pushed into the middle water;
a V-shaped current pushed outward behind us
and the sun deposited gold onto the breaking
miniature waves. And while the motor spoke,
we stopped searching for words.

Perhaps we fished as an obligation to custom
that began long before I held a fishing rod.
A father, remembering trips with his own dad,
could hold out hope that a remembered joy of his own
past trips could pass between them through the calm.

And I, whose thoughts often lived miles away,
knew it was right to try but failed at hiding
a yawn, or morning shivers. Soon the sun
would rise and turn to summer sweat.

One spot on the lake looked as good as any
For now. The mechanical act of casting
We learned from somewhere: a backward glance,
A hook safely dangled away from flesh,
Cast forward with the flick of a wrist.

As the lure flew the sound of tension disappeared
And a thumb snapped down the metal ring,
felt the line reach its limit, the bait splash down.

As the sun rose, and the heat, we turned
to the shrinking shadows, casting toward
a waterlogged tree (close without snagging)
where fish would gather.
                      All day long
we followed this pattern, warming, cooling,
chasing shadows, staring at floats for some
evidence of the unseen.

Across the lake, rare sights of other boats,
and even rarer sounds of words,
barbed hooks sticking in the mind.

DESERT SUN

Getting Clean in Basic

At eighteen, you take your first plane ride
toward nine weeks of hell. First stop, Nashville,
where technicians take your blood,
take your piss, confer in whispered tones.
Finally a Staff Sergeant hands you a ticket
to Columbia. First time you've been this high
off the ground.
                              Oh, you've been high before.
Hours before, you flushed a bottle
of Percocets down the drain, and now
everything hurts—your back curved
into the crescent seat, your arms having
bumped every metal chairback you passed
walking toward your fate through a cattle chute.

You knew it would hurt worse when the bird
landed.
                    Rumors of the way drills would line
fresh recruits up, inspecting people
like cuts of meat, linger. You try to take your mind
off of it, look at the curves of the middle-aged stewardess
and think of a woman you know back home,
the look you two shared in those moments
of clarity upon passing her house—
you sweating through your jogging clothes,
her clipping roses, looking up and waving
in skimpy shorts. You wonder if she'll be there
when you return, if you'll be bigger.

You used to think there'd always be tomorrow.
And now, higher than ever before, you know tomorrow
is no given. The days, the shouting, pass like blurs.
The nights you freeze the stewardess's image
in your mind as if a distant lover
with a make-believe heartache—all while lying
on top of a wool blanket, ninety-two degrees
in the dead chill of night, stiff blanket fibers
stabbing your skin and the forced sobriety—
can help subdue the feeling of arms sore
from a hundred incorrect pushups
and road-march-sausaged feet.

It is here, in this moth-eaten mattress
where the muscles melt, that you think

you've died. And that thought makes the shouting,
the raw nerve on the edge of jagged bone,
the seared skin and fire ants, makes it livable.

You'll rise when the drill flips on the sun;
you'll try to give what rises a new name.

But for now you think of her—the closest thing to high
you'll have in these last moments in the dark—while lying,
waiting for the light, checking your watch, counting
backwards from four a.m.—that moment when a daily dose
of urgency chases the pain and the fog away.

Transubstantiation

When a convoy pulls inside the wire
without a tragic roadside stop,
a soldier takes grape Gatorade,
still cold from the refrigerated truck,
and holds it to his steaming face.

Another carries a bottle to the chaplain
who's lining through his notes. He wipes
sweat from his head and stares at the duct
pumping lukewarm air beneath chapel walls,
once a hangar and, yesterday, a gym.

Soldiers drape white tablecloth over metal
plates, and the priest pours the drink
into a makeshift flagon. Another hand
turns on the tape of organ music.

That's his cue. Almost forty faces stare down,
or straight ahead, or into space.
They've worn their cleanest uniforms
and wiped dust from molded rifle stocks,
the barrels all pointed safely toward the back.

"They need something to believe," he thinks.
A hundred twenty degrees fades,
if only for an hour. Purple cools the ad hoc chalice.
A soldier sips, and sweetness washes sand
from the dry recesses of his mouth.

Retreat

I.

Redness invades a soldier's face
after the vise of crossed arms closes
against the cracked proving ground.
Still, it surprises me. We practice
the chokes, the pressure points, the things
I hope we will never use. My hands grip
his collar from the inside
in that textbook way so my arms
can cross, scissor-like, cutting air.

"Switch places!" booms the instructor's voice,
and my head rests now near a black
fire ant mound. It is only a matter of time
before the invaded army swarms.

My partner grabs, pulls, crosses,
and while I'm staring upward,
the white sky blinds until air vanishes
and the world turns black again.

II.

On another country's unforgiving earth,
one hand learns to rest on the trigger well.
The other hand rehearses: grab, pull, cross.
Oil-black eyes follow me, never quite
meeting mine. Children stare from open doors
at my neck. School has been closed six years
and I have become their text.
These days they have only time: watch, study, wait.

Even the ground, where beneath doorways
a camel spider drags the larger lizard
in its jaw, strives to take a man's breath away.

III.

The house that welcomes me now
feels foreign, as if ceramic tile
threatens to crack beneath my soles
that still carry grains of sand.

Outside the screen door, a moth
breaks its body against the porch light.
For a second, I think of catching the moth
body between thumb and forefinger
and pressing the life out. It's what I know.
Instead, I interlock my fingers and turn away.

In our bedroom, you stretch
half-naked across our mattress.
"Why do you never sleep here?"
I can only shrug while looking at your neck,
knowing where each vein and artery rest.

I wander off, another night drawn
to the glow of blue television light,
hands under my folded arms. I know
these hands wait for a more useful task.

Sestina for Landstuhl Nurses

An Army transport from Balad emerges above the tree line,
and as it descends another night bleeds into another morning.
In minutes a quiet German drive will become the sound of steel,
the peal of sirens. A nurse looks up from her car. For now, peace.
She composes letters in her mind, the words of a mother
to her son, somewhere over there, not knowing what waits to explode.

And then the grinding as a bus engine revs and sound explodes
on the Autobahn. The ambulance weaves around a line
of morning traffic, and through glass windows a mother
sees sons and daughters on canvas cots. The morning
starts early; she floors the gas and follows. Now, peace
is only last night's dream that foreign bullets conspire to steal.

The corridors are clean from last night's work, but she will steel
herself for passing parents who wait. What dreams of youth explode.
Her walk to the scrub sink grows, and she wrings her hands. "Peace
be with you," leaves her lips before she crosses the sterile line,
and it matters these families believe that she believes. Repeated mornings
have not made it easier—each has a mother

waiting for news—and she hopes they never do. A boy on the table. "Mother
fucker shot himself," a medic rolls his eyes. One hand grips the steel
table edge; another preps—no time for contempt, or even mourning.
She mutters, "What pushed him to the brink? Did pressure build, explode?
Was it hearing 'Suck it up' one final time?" There's a line
between mission and human. If anyone knew where, would it bring peace?

Dressings that held him together on a five-hour flight fall, then a piece
of him. It is here she knows the fear of every mother,
what she never saw when her boy's hand signed along the line.
The surgeon's staff has learned to hum through horror and over steel
hitting the floor, white noise of suction. Bone saw chatters, explodes.
Eighteen years dissolve in three-second tragedies. It is still morning.

Nurses peel the hour's work into red bags. A speaker blasts, "Sunday morning
chapel," and medics push the stretcher to Recovery where a fragile peace
remains. It will not last. Soon electric-powered doors will explode
and end the short respite. More families fill the waiting room, a mother
"to which boy on which bed?" The nurse turns toward them, steals
a cuppa joe, and walks to where they wait. She wants to talk, but there's a line.

It's only eight a.m. and, still, charts lie in a growing line.
A surgeon screams he'll explode if someone doesn't prep his room. "Mother,"
she sighs in the morning hour, walks to the next case in a moment of peace.

Blackhawk Crash

Bone-weary eyes scanned the soil and sky for the corner flash
of tracer rounds, night in, night out. The rotor's muffled hum
betrayed a darkened metal blended against the black
or, overhead, the searchlight's crescent sweep.

Smitty scanned while Cote fought sleep in the firing port
and the Blackhawk flew past chain link fence and razor wire,
like any night, before desert air raised its fearful blanket
of dust and spinning sand, blotting out the stars.

Darkness overtook machine, reduced its inner flesh
to a scent of burning oil, a motor seized, and the hot breath
of a black tail spinning over facedown soldiers
who crouched and waited for the blade to strike.

Seconds stretched to seeming hours before the bird, sideways,
sent the first blade snapping against the desert floor
with fist-like echoes. Only the crew, voices swallowed by chindi,
stayed silent
        in the spinning, words pulled from flesh.

Unspoken names remained muffled in an eddy of debris. The dust
devil hands turned backward, snapping each life taut.

As the sun rose, a Kevlar helmet lay upright in breaking light
half a mile from the wreckage, a ghost bead loosed
from its string and, without ceremony,
                returned to earth.

KBR Shower

Long past the graveyard shift the sentry,
relieved of his post, begins the walk
toward a shower and a cot.

The white trailers look the same this time of night
save stenciled numbers barely read. He allows
his eyes to focus in the still-safe center of the wire.

Rifle hanging from a dirty sling, the soldier stops
to smoke beside a concrete wall where the day's sun
has gathered, waiting for its escape. Invisible,
the heat blasts high from the side, draws a bead
of sweat from beneath his cap.

He relishes the dead-calm quiet on nights free
of mortar rounds; small arms fire
beats a rhythmic dance from the valley.
The generator's mono-roar has become the sweating
white noise that drowns unwanted thoughts,
letting those not lying in the dirt sleep.

He walks up metal steps to the empty shower point,
leans his rifle, pulls sandals, soap, a mildewed towel
from his pack; he strips the day, layer by layer,
and finds the deeper places where dust still manages
to paste itself.
                    Then comes the water's hum
and he knows—three minutes of heat to work
out the knots. Eyes closed, he imagines the hand
running across his scalp to be his wife's

until the electric pulse runs from the drain
and up his leg and through his chest.

There is no bottom to the apathy
some feel for the rest.

The Mortar's Whistle

Around a makeshift grill, soldiers' faces
turn into red crescents. Only a jawline,
or the slightest shift of rifle barrels, catches
firelight, betrays men camouflaged outside its glow.

Stolen mess hall chicken cooks on a metal drum.
The bird skin, unlike the human kind,
takes its own sweet time browning over flame.

"My wife," says one. "My boy," says another,
pouring a mix of GI spice we call gunpowder.
Pepper cracks in red coals and flashes skyward.

A klaxon sounds and two newbies drop facedown.
We watch the speed with which they fall,
remain standing, hurl F bombs at the sky.

We turn silent when the whistle passes.
Then we turn the meat, because

if tonight's our last supper,
damn if we're going to let it burn.

The Fearmongers

This morning someone lost his head across
the globe, except the sun was setting there.
We watched it from the breakfast counter while
a waitress filled our cups. One marveled how
this masked marauder showed resolve,
and wouldn't it be swell if leaders here
committed to a course with half the zeal.
I thought I recognized a rock formation on
the screen, the spot the man in orange knelt.
I walked around that place or one just like it.
Another man spoke, he'd "never go quietly,"
and why we didn't send an army in.
It made no sense. A man who wore a VFW hat
just looked and shook his head, then turned away.
The eyes on the screen revealed nothing except
a cold psychotic stare;
                              the picture took
me back to when I'd watch the black and whites.
Once, *The Invisible Man* was on, the shape
of a man but wrapped in bandages, with shades,
and when he peeled the layers off it gave
me chills. Some nights I'd lie awake and listen;
with every subtle noise my voice would rasp,
"Who's there?" We're wondering that now; the man-
shaped mask begins to follow us everywhere.

Outside, the day is getting hot. The blood-
red moon that blazed above the diner's roof
has all but faded. This morning, walking in,
we marveled in the quiet; then someone flipped
on the *idiot* box. Breakfast over and paid for,
the crew spills out. We're making small talk to fill
the void until we reach our separate cars.
Each one becomes suspicious, walking
in a man-shaped mask—unsure what lies beneath

Theseus in Baghdad

Climbing the metal steps of the 747, he thought to turn, as if he could see her standing in the sand, becoming smaller. Of course she was tending someone else by now, weapon racked, body armor stashed in a corner somewhere, in a converted Baghdad school. The patients kept coming, but maybe she looked up into the sky from time to time. What labyrinthine troubles, lost in the dark alleys and unmarked streets. He remembered a wrong turn and what the IED left behind; remembered he'd never seen such a tangled mess of limbs. Half-men, he thought. And she standing over him next, him waking, her tying him back together with string. "You're a godsend," he told her and thought, once, he saw a tear. But she had other guys to stitch, to bring out of a dark sleep, and so he never asked. But he wondered, times like now, looking down to see land diminish, then looking up where space stretched above the wings like a long black sail.

Shooting Silhouettes

A man-made berm rises behind twenty wooden frames,
and in those frames sit paper targets, tubes that taper
at the top. If we're surrounded by anonymous
black shapes with no neck, we'll be prepared.
A voice from the tower says "fire," and so we do,
without question. Forty shots pepper each silhouette
and, when we're done, we stare through smoke,
squinting and trying to count the beams of light
shining through the black, trying to know the score first.
Someone cracks, "Everyone's an expert when they
ain't shootin' back." Someone else says, "I'll just imagine
black silhouettes, no face, no neck,

                            and do just fine."

Old War Movies and the News

As kids, we watched actors charge up Pork Chop Hill. Each shot, it sounded
like popcorn, and when the soldiers fell, it seemed like play. Behind the sofa
where we leaned toward our tiny screen, a friend blew up a paper bag with air
and popped it with his open hand. No one jumped. Someone shot a dirty look;
there were fistfuls of kernels that flew like shrapnel. But most would focus
on the scene as minor characters fell like bowling pins, then reset when the
screen went dark. That's how we learned about battle. A few years later, a new
war hit the six o-clock news. We'd eat in silence, watching round white dots fall
into geometries we learned were buildings: the small white dots blew shit up—
black squares in videogame crosshairs. We'd watch the ordnance drop—bloodless—
reverse its course and rise, only to drop again. A decade passed, and now
we wait in the desert to board the trucks—fresh uniforms feel so damned crisp.
Ironed edges create clean lines. While we're waiting, three quick bursts
crash through the air.
        It will be the last time nobody moves.

Overwatch

"Stay watchful," he says to no one, to the eyes
that would watch, fighting sleep in the intersection
      of blood and dust.

Friendlies pass with a glance toward the crest
and a false smile that means, "don't shoot."

Rakes, shovels and Soviet-made rifles peek
      from a truck bed.
It is the others, eyes down, resolute,
who conceal a day's labor beneath a tarp
and stare into a field of ochre where an

unseen hand smears the horizon. An index
      finger touches cold metal.

* * *

Many days the trucks never come and the desert
stretches bare; this time the sunset's long red arms
will not reveal some hidden pressure plate
and the figure in his sights becomes her—

his voice he imagines is hers. In this version,
she bakes warm bread, her hands flatten and knead,
and the dough is the parched earth.

His is the voice saying, "lock up before bed time"
or, worried of some faceless man who tarries on
the sidewalk in front, he says, "keep walking."

* * *

In June, he flew home and, among family become
strangers, he saw these crossroads in his mind,
and the explosions of each six o'clock cycle
ate a hole that home-cooked bread
      could never fill,

and she could sense the barometer's drop and switched
the television off, as if, in not hearing,
"nobody dies, they are only sleeping."

Still, he scanned the sand through a small silver screen,
past a toddler stacking blocks, past a reporter's moving lips,
into the blackened shell of an American truck.

* * *

A soldier returns to his promontory to find himself
thinking of home, stopping to give names
to the lizard, to the scorpion, who share the rocky soil
        like old friends.

In these days, when the road remains clear, he prays
or pulls the day's letter,
a "mail order soul," from his pack

and reads in silent dusk. The only sign of life—
steam rises from sunbaked cracks,
one eye on the road below, one eye—

he pictures a room; he pictures her.
And he's hoping the next time he's standing there,
the room is large enough to hold all of him.

Negative Space

Again
it's two a.m.
Fresh linens roll themselves
into a garrote, or the body
beneath an avalanche
of white sand, and there is only
this end
and the other.

At two a.m.,
the mattress forms a crater
and sleep becomes
a trench warfare of its own.
For seconds, the body
finds a cool corner of bed,
and drifts, until dreams
of desert sun and terra-cotta
carry me out.

That's the time
you look my way smiling.
I can never understand what
there is to smile about, and then
you turn your head. Red petals
open into full blossom,
an exit wound in the back
of your mind.
Your smile becomes a vacant
beam, and air stumbles,
rasping, over a bone cage
in its hurry to leave.

It is sunny in the desert,
and my wife's two a.m.
voice asks who I'm talking
to. She lays spooned
against a shifting dune.

"I think my ride is here," you say,
and then the whirring rotors confirm.

It's two a.m.,
and the unmistakable blades
of a Blackhawk slice through
the air. A brass chain
scrapes in the blades.
Your voice from the rotor
asks me, in machine-gun rhythm,
to save it—

and I'm falling upward.

Let It Burn

*Though the military says trash taken to the Balad pit is sorted
before it is burned, visits to the pit earlier this year revealed
closed trash bags being thrown in the pit and partly burned
metal drums and aerosol cans among the rubble.*
—Stars and Stripes, Nov. 7, 2008

Let it burn, the litany of letters,
Dear John, Dear Jane, there's no polite way
to say "go fuck yourself."
Flames lick and the ink turns blacker in the air.

Let it burn, the misplaced medical chart,
where Private D's two cracked disks will keep him
from retiring from the only job he's loved,
but not until the next mission and the next
and the next. For riding gunner on a cratered street,
he's just good enough.

Let it burn, a sustainable plan to train the locals.
The lesson turns orange, then black,
dumped by cynics who still say "hearts and minds"
but now don't bother to hide the smirk.

Let it burn, Lieutenant C's laptop yesterday left alone
on a tailgate. He can't for the life of him remember
whose job it was to watch it, and the hundred
suicide prevention numbers and charts turn to ash.

Let it burn, the investigation—the words and witness
of Staff Sergeant V, who pushed his way into her trailer;
let burn the kit, the chart, the bruises on film,
and the counselor's report—all swept
from the corner. "He's one of my best,"
and the Colonel wipes his hands.

Let it burn, Master Sergeant's Bronze Star
flung from behind his trailer in the dark;
the five points will no longer stick in his skin.
Not to mention plastic cans with an inch of diesel,
unmarked chemicals. "Make this disappear,"
someone said, and someone did.

Specialist M holds a kerchief to his face with his left,
stokes the fire with his right, wondering what lies dying
in the flame, while the smoke rises around and through him,
beginning its slow resurrection from inside his lungs.

Atrocity

Some nights when the world is asleep, I open the file on my computer
and scroll one by one through pictures of Iraq. Most are battered
buildings, towers, mosques, a sheet metal roof with the nose
of a mortar peeking through. But the one I stare at most is a boy,
maybe a teen, standing in a line of men, face crisscrossed
by a chain-link fence. He's waiting to come on post for work,
one brown eye, one socket. My own eyes keep tracing the red
empty oval, socket still wet. The lower lid sags; the top lid not enough
to cover the emptiness. I remember other wounds, a stub cleaved
just above the wrist, a pants leg folded in half, safety-pinned
at the owner's hip. I don't know why I caught this photo or kept it,
or what happened. Some nights I'd ask the soldiers coming back
who'd spent a day supervising work details (we called them LNs)
how it went. Some would shrug, some'd say "waste of day."
One would joke that these men speaking different languages
could never follow directions. I don't know what I wanted to hear—
maybe that someone saw a wound from which they couldn't turn away,
or saw something human. I don't know what happened to the eye
whose empty red socket stared back at me, whose bullet took the eye,
what I even saw, or why I'm writing it down.

RETURNING TO THE HILL COUNTRY

Domestic Dogs Running Loose

No one seems to understand what dogs
at night are chasing, if the night itself
will turn these dogs to something wild
with longer teeth, a keener smell.

Four sets of amber eyes peer out from a copse
of cedar trees betrayed by headlight beams.
A driver turning on an ess-shaped curve
ignores the sight his headlights catch, sweeping

through a neighbor's field, exposing them.
A fool ignores these wild domestics, thinking a collar
a sign of domesticity. "Lock your fence,
and keep 'em fed, your dogs won't run."

But there's the corpse of a calf now rotting
on the furthest hill, a chicken found outside
its coop, a smaller dog—a neighbor's terrier
that bolted one night, long after dinner

scraps were scraped. It ran through the yard
into the woods and never was seen again.
These bodies lay uneaten, an urge
that's deeper than reason.
                            Driving to Fort Hood,
a night without sleep has left me red-eyed awake.
My mind is running across fencerows. I drive
on autopilot where a formation of troops waits,
where, still, it is dark. Without thinking, I count

soldiers who stand waiting for the clock to strike
at six, for the cannon fire. There's forty here,
which means for now that no one has been arrested
for answering the call of a human wild, where clubs

sell booze to minors sporting fresh tattoos
they purchased with a payday loan. And all
of them, for one night, avoided fighting
the enemy outside the gates.
                            It would be easy
to claim some speech I said still lingered in
their minds. But traveling the darkest fields where roads
and headlights never reach, the message seems
to take a twisting path that reason can't.

The Foyer of a Soldier's House

Returning is false happiness.

Before he left, world and belief collided
in a rustic foyer that lay between them.
An eye filtered the world and a man who stood
on a manicured lawn with his wife, laughing,
could only see dark green Bermuda,
never the black soil below,

and the soldier carried that vision over dry rock,
up brick towers, onto the roofs of Baghdad.
He trained his eye in a barren land
to see the slightest change; darker soil
signaled buried pressure plates.

Or maybe the sound of a pebble
kicked by a rubber sole, the sound of metal springs
falling from tire tread and skittering across asphalt.
Each nerve stretched like piano wire awaiting
the hammer's fall.

A whisper became an explosion,
and the world pushed inward, lingering in the doorway.

Now the last rifle has been racked,
the last boot tucked, and to the prodigal
the house becomes so quiet, a key sliding through metal
becomes a 5.56 ball entering a bone-dry chamber.

A roomful of voices blends into the static
of late night radio gone out of range.

The right frequency gains entry:
a light switch snaps, an ornament falls and shatters,
a car engine revs in the distance.

It takes effort to realize bright lights on the highway
are not signal flares. In time, the noise fades
and familiar voices rise out of the static;
green grass stems rise out of the soil.

Holy City of the Wichitas

Beneath the ground, a fault line runs
between granite slabs that still manage
to break the surface here and there,

rising above tall grass and scrub oak,
like this path where men have shaped
cobblestone into a stage,

a palace, a court, an upper room,
a tax collector's house, stable and an inn.
A gift shop sits beside a gaudy sign

that no one tries to hide.
The mind makes its own passion play.
We step to the edge of the gravel path—

from here the prairie grass tosses in waves.
A boy has climbed the ruins
of a weathered fishing boat.

The boat leans, having never touched water.
The boy jumps; his head sinks below the grass.
Someone shouts, "Oh look at that!"

while a lady, alone, hand over her eyes,
implores the boy to come back
up the hill.

Most seem
to smile at a child being a child
for a few more years.

We walk to the end of the set,
forget the chaos, stop where
three hulking roods

hover above the mountain range—
timbers tall beyond reason
in a place whose tallest tree

can be no more than a half-century old.
Yet there they stand, empty, allowing
minds to make their own miracle.

Beyond the beaten path,
three bison graze in a sea of bluestem,
never looking up.

Maundy Thursday, Fort Hood, Texas

We first learned the ritual as children,
the way hands carried water without spilling,
the way our chaplain washed another's feet;
no one ever questioned it.

The way hands carried water without spilling,
this cold spring night just chilled us.
No one ever questioned it
until we saw this act of kindness in the flesh.

This cold spring night just chilled us.
We never thought removing shoes so hard
until we saw this act of kindness in the flesh.
Grown men wept, the sight of a leader kneeling.

We never thought removing shoes so hard.
Thirty minutes ago there'd been only laughter.
Grown men wept, the sight of a leader kneeling.
The Last Supper some strange tale we'd heard.

Thirty minutes ago there'd been only laughter,
before this ritual we'd learned as children.
The Last Supper was only some strange tale we'd heard,
before we saw the chaplain wash another's feet.

Steer

Driving home, a red taillight wake hung in the air.
A moonless night cloaked the overpass, its presence betrayed
by the interstate hum. Neither crickets nor drenched country
air clinging to an open window made a sound.

Southward, the honeyed glow of city lights
covered the horizon like fading embers;
a calligraphy of cattle dotted black hills.

These beacons I remembered, navigating by the remembered
rise and fall, leaning into each embankment by feel,
drunk with the smell of sassafras, lilac and cowshit.

The last working speaker rasped, lulling me to dreams.
"What color is black when it burns?" A voice drifted
from the dashboard before something blacker, a steer,
stomped through an unseen fence to reach sweet grass and thistle.
A purple bloom still hung from its jaw and twin beams
reflected back from a wide ebon pool before the car
skidded past in a late-night slide without witness.

Simple. A conical sweep of headlights, empty road; steer
left to a soft gravel shoulder, then home with another word to keep.

Years later this rough beast wakes a man, stomach pressed
against ribs, recalling: brake pedal, petrified fish hook fingers,
the smell of perfumed shit, and twin headlights reflecting from the dark
glassy eye of a twelve hundred pound steer—whether such a sight
is possible or not—still chewing that thistle, no jump, no scream.

One sense recalls the others and a nonsense song,
"What color is black when it burns?"

There are times, in the still dark hours, I almost know.

Mousetrap

The thwack in the night shatters sleep,
echoes on the other side of a plaster and pine
two by four wall, which I've learned does little
to block out sound. Rather, it carries
voices:
      like a mother and father who remove
their brave faces each midnight
while itemizing what's left for groceries
and shoes; or a breakup in a Motel 6
punctuated by an alarm clock smashing
into bits against our shared wall
in some small town I will pass through
and never remember its name.

Tonight, I've settled into the first house
I've owned, bleary-eyed from thunderstorms.
There are rubbery mouse feet drumming
across an oak bench, magnified in the wall's
empty spaces. I can only imagine the damage
done by small teeth burrowing outside-in.
He wants to escape the rain that's rising
in the backyard. For a few minutes I wonder
if a small trail of brown pellets is reason
enough to exterminate—until the final
spring-loaded snap pierces
the hollows of the wall between us.
And all other images—of poverty, of loneliness,
of destruction—recede, if only for the night.

Mapmaking

With an empty page, a boy begins to build.
Thumb and forefinger swing the nib like shovel and pick
and, in the wake, a sea of black forms the world.
Lines waver, asymmetric, into battered shores—

and soon the line turns, turns again, and closes upon itself;
beginning meets end, earth rises, and the ink-dark sea falls.

Random towns appear, and hills marked by contour lines;
blue river runs through center, then fans into a delta.
An occasional boat leaves no trace, nor the fanged sea
serpent the boy has drawn to mark the paper's edge.

Soon, color arrives. These right-angled roads form silver
boundaries, apply order to unruly trees and the green anarchy
of grass. Finally, the small hand sprinkles the world—
rectangle buildings and stick men stand in parallel, stick arms open—

and when he sees that it is good, he carries his world
to the kitchen table where the adults have kept busy
speaking of news while slicing, storing summer's last harvest
of wild tomatoes into Mason jars. Before anyone can stop

its fall, the world on paper sinks to the wooden surface,
only to have the red of freshly cut fruit rise through its center.

One Evening in Early Spring

The visible remains of another day are evident as grey light
above treetops. Shadows have swallowed the back-yard;
our white salamander friend arrives, climbing to the soffit
upside down. A feral cat's outline emerges against the sky
on the corner fence post. The small gods are waking.

An owl, known only by the breeze of its wings, passes
and an opossum ambles through a patch of windowlight.
We step out the back door, no flashlight, silent in our deck
chairs at the edge of the porch. The kids race into the dark,
positions betrayed only by the sound of laughter. I, having slowed
with age, close my eyes, listening for evidence: the cat racing
away, the neighbor dog barking, followed by another dog
in the distance. This way we map our known world.
The kids ask us to come play, and so we move into the night.
In time our eyes adjust. Outside the electric light's radius,
we begin to see it, the not being alone, the way bodies
under the moon begin to illuminate, the ivy, the sharp grass blades—

until a siren splinters the air, and red light blinds us all.

Compline

After the last prayer for peaceful night,
the congregation spills down the concrete steps
blazing white in electric light.
Spring's metal chill washes over a skin
grown tired of clinging to jawbones, eye sockets
and fretful fingers.
                              Bodies scatter into the dark;
the white noise of worry fades. Even the urge to war,
the reliving of some harsh word bubbling
beneath this human husk, begins to still.
                                            Across the globe,
it is eight hours ahead, and bombs are still falling.
A father's lifting concrete fragments, following
the sound of the voices.
                              In the makeshift parking lot,
a mother clutches her child's hand;

they're searching for their car, walking
carefully on dark grass. We keep walking
away from the distractions, farther
to the edge of civilization.
                              Cassiopeia,
to the north, reveals herself to the eye.
Here we can look up, connecting ourselves
to the stars, without scurrying for cover.
Cricket song rises from the tall weeds.
Shapes we've never seen beyond the pale
of city light emerge. We walk into the dead calm,
away from small talk and politics.

We're following the voices. We find ourselves
between the straight shafts of sycamore trees,

and bodies become smooth white fire.

Three Battles in the Hill Country

I.

Back of a rented house, its mock barn roof
warps; paint peels from the eave.

Feeders suspend from what branches remain,
while the severed limbs claim squatter's rights
by the gravel drive. Residue of an evening

thunderstorm gathers in a dead fountain;
bees reclaim the basin's edge
where water pools amid cracks and, above,
a plaster Neptune fondles a fish.

The white pine lattice hangs
on a climbing rose, still standing but fallen
so far behind on the rent she no longer cares.

Survivors of the rain season find ways to sleep.

II.

Rains in the hill country create transient
lakes. A neglected Folgers can defines
water into a cylinder; months of frustration

bleed a ferrous beck through its seam.

Fireflies light on the skin of water maple leaves,
unafraid for the first time in years of Mason jars.

Toad hangs from the storm door, a presence
so silent until,
                    in a flash,
his X-ray outline burns into the dark.

Then,
        thunderclap!

In the quieting aftermath, Cricket
strokes her thigh without rosin,
moving Bullfrog to stutter.

The improvisation of the wild drowns
an interstate's protracted groan one mile away.

III.

Television's blue flashes expose ivy skeletons
covering window panes, and beneath the sill

a headless prickly pear rises.

A lone pickup truck sits empty on half–flat tires
where honeysuckle sags over the fencerow
like a warning.
                    The owner of the house no longer
ventures past the door, a casualty of a lost war.

Foxes

Beyond the fence, the fog rises slowly
up from the cove, a mountain witches' brew.
There's a rustle in the scrub oak;
behind it an unseen sun shapes the world,
gleams off the metal fence that exists
to keep us from plummeting
off the edge.
          Without warning, a mother fox
and three kits emerge. The mother steps
slowly into the clearing, shakes off the dew,
and turns.
         She cannot protect them
from what comes next: hawks, farmers,
lawmen—each fearful of their dark bodies.

The children copy, shaking, freezing;
four sets of eyes stare across an open field.

I watch, hot coffee steam rising from the cup.
When she notices me, she bares her teeth
and I, the intruder, do not move.

Asymptote

It's when we lie awake at night
the darkness rises almost to our skin
and, if we're still, we quiet the fictive
beasts of our anxieties, feel it sprawl,
and now it's not so wild. The night has taken
nearly human form; and we, so spent
from worry, push against the room,
find nothing pushing back—a thought
that comforts us. With that, the beastly
sounds begin to vanish. We roll
over, cool, and let the night cover us;
the moon and stars almost touch our skin.

Callouses

While we're lying in the dark, she notices
identical rough callouses on the edges
of both hands.

                I mean, in years of working
behind a desk, these hands, they still remember
the unforgiving *smooth* of the tomahawk-shaped
tobacco knife. Then, the left hand would push
the six-foot stalk to the ground; the right hand
would cleave it just above the root. So long as I cut
below the bottom leaf, that was money.

And by the end of a row, skin beneath the pinky
opened and tobacco juice stung. The left hand would
be black with tar save a small burning red patch;
the right hand would be shaped like a grappling hook.
And sometimes, tired, I would switch hands
to see if I could, taking some extra whacks while men
in adjacent rows would shake their heads.
                          Now, some days,
rising from an early morning bed, or on Sundays
taking a bow before the altar, I feel the catch in my back
remind me of where I'm from; I feel the weight of the plant,
its gum-coated leaves, remember grabbing it with two
hands to spear the stalk on the hickory stick.
                          Back then,
when I'd finish a row, my dad would be halfway through the next.
Or, he'd wait to say "better stay in school, this ain't for you."

And, for a minute, we would stare up our own crooked rows
and past the edges into tall grass where our thoughts
would stay until the sun, burning our necks,
woke us, returned us to a world that wouldn't fix itself.

This morning, light creeps around the corner of blackout
drapes; the air cycles on and exhales from the vent
across smooth shoulders. It's getting hot outside.
I rub my hand across her back, let the rough patch drag
for just a second or two, telling her who I am
better this way than I can do with words.

Nine Hundred Miles

Nine hundred miles ago I knew a man—
we walked the fields; we'd seldom speak.
He'd stare into an approaching dark. I used to stand

the way he stood, tiptoeing to take a peek.
That's how boys would learn from silent men.
We'd walk the fields; we'd seldom speak.

Our chores, the hay, the crops, all kept us busy then,
and when I'd tire he'd keep on going.
That's how boys learned from silent men.

Last time we talked, I wasn't the same boy growing
up in his house. We pointed out each other's mistakes
and when I tired he'd still be going.

Nine hundred miles to drive and think. My head aches.
I wonder what conspiracy's got him wound up now.
Up in his house, we pointed out each other's mistakes.

Nine hundred miles I hoped the memory'd fade, somehow,
but I'm staring at approaching darkness, trying to make a stand.
I wonder what conspiracy's got him wound up now—
if he's staring at the approaching dark where we used to stand.

Come Winter

Low-lying clouds are stifling street sounds.
Cars, absent from driveways; front doors stay
shut; blackout screens cling to the home fronts.
The town grows more silent, plainer. An engine revs
somewhere beyond a slate-grey rooftop.
Or someone is burning trash, or burning a house—
or it's that rare glimpse when we see
a soul depart.
              Inside the back garden, furrows
have hardened to frozen scars. The last tomato vine
sags over its wire cage, then stiffens in fixed
spasm. Blackberry briars turn wooden,
their rust-colored spikes exposed.
                           Blood has slowed;
color has faded—each withdrawn into its own healing.
Within this cavernous house, only a clock pendulum
moves, each ticking gear tooth a light step toward
some horizon. Dry fingers release the venetian blinds;
eyes shut. An internal chant keeps pace
with the pendulum—*beware...beware*—
with the gunpowder volley through artery walls.
In solitary thought, the voice becomes
repair...repair—eyes shut, and winter comes.

Love in the Time of Hysteria

Tonight, love will be difficult.
—Nathalie Handal

We sit close, but without touching; a thousand flickering
images pass through the screen. A hand stretches toward another,
stopping just short. A woman makes fists in front
of a pile of rubble, and though we can't understand her words,
we know. Anyone who ever knew someone who's lost knows.
Anyone not turned to piles of stone. Tonight, who has a right
to risk bringing life into this? The images shift—
flashing blue lights, twisted metal, the angry eyes
and stiff lips of fearful men, a Glock here, a Bushmaster
there, refugee fingers wrapped around chain link, and flags,
an abundance of flags. Mothers show premature
wrinkles without shame. Sirens lure the fearful men
into the rocks. Tonight, with effort, the hands find
each other. It's the job before us, the not turning to stone.

A HANDFUL OF DUST

Our House Is Alarmed

Our house is alarmed the day the salesman knocks.
He wants to sell security. To close
the deal, he turns, looks through the cul-de-sac,
and questions how well we know the neighborhood.

What's with the man who's slinking out, who takes
the Friday paper while holding his bathrobe closed?
Or Mrs. Frazier mowing grass, suspicious
in shades? And now the blue rubber wastebin
casts long shadows; the mailbox leans away;
and children's games become a code for—what?

Even the house murmurs through its vents.
The wall's tremble keeps time with the salesman's pitch;
windows slyly avert their gaze; and the door,
sensing that nothing will be the same, slams shut.

Villanelle for Charleston

We're waiting for the bells to ring at nine.
A crowd has gathered at the chapel door
to mark these lives or curse the dark divine.

These strangers give a wary look, benign
but tense. No one feels safe here anymore.
We're waiting for the bells to ring at nine.

Of all the cares we thought we'd left behind,
we thought this place was safe; but, pacing floors,
we're marking lives, we're cursing the divine.

Here someone reads the news; the day's headline—
the lone gunman lie—it chills us to the core
while waiting for the bells to ring at nine.

Scripture, perhaps, will help. I wrack my mind,
but nothing helps—not silent prayers nor
us marking lives or cursing the divine.

We're standing here outside; a growing line
surrounds the marble steps of this chapel where
we're marking lives, not cursing the divine.
We're waiting while the bells still ring for nine.

Southern Prayers

Lame, wrinkled, cross-eyed, they try to follow
behind Folly, who, because she's strong and quick,
runs far in front of them, appearing
all over the world, bringing harm to men.
Far behind, Prayers carry on their healing.
—The Iliad. IX. 629-633.

Three prayers cross an empty street,
eyes downcast against December wind;
they whisper as they walk, "Blessed are the Meek,"

past tinderbox stores, parked cars with empty seats.
Windows blaze their brightest on the sun's descent
while three prayers cross an empty street.

How easily small towns mistake meek for weak,
and Folly laughs, thinking everything is evident.
They whisper as they walk, "Blessed are the Meek";

they pass a thigh-high fireplug that sits discrete,
that holds water's metric tons in its fist.
Three prayers cross an empty street

with the tale of burned-out churches, water's bleak
memory of steam, or bone cleaved from skin,
yet they whisper as they walk, "Blessed are the Meek."

Pressure builds darkly under concrete,
where rivers rage to be with other rivers, intent
that pious women not forget, "Blessed are the Meek"
uttered in prayers rising up from empty streets.

Dog Whistle

The ghost of another workday rises through the subdivision.
A music of deadbolt locks punctuates the air, and the evening
darkens with the drawing of the shades.

Drivers find themselves alone. Raised windows protect
against the scent of magnolia, skunk and smoke,
while the music of tire treads, of distant sirens, drowns in a sea
of late-night radio.
                        One such solitary man gropes blindly
at the dash. The road dims in the corner of his eye, while a finger
reaches for the sound, turns the knob until a voice emerges.

The DJ says the word *alien,* and the driver, hearing a familiar pitch,
stops his tuning and veers into the parking lot of a 7-Eleven.

The cigarettes can wait. Caller and radio jock are really going
at it, their shared narrative of crime and fences.
Yes, he thinks, and his grip tenses on the steering wheel.

Boys have gathered beneath the flashing Miller High Life sign,
gesturing with empty hands. They flash razor-white
teeth, and their easy laughter makes it hard to hear.
He turns the volume louder and seethes inside the fiberglass
prison.
        Now his hands won't operate the door.

He tells himself to hold his chin high. "Don't show it," he says
only to himself; he would steel himself to walk past
what stares he can only imagine, but his legs won't move.

In the gleam of a white fluorescent bulb that bounces
off a pair of eyes, he sees and, when he sees,

his mind travels to his house behind a deadbolt lock,
his pantry stocked, his precious collections, his wife
in her gown reading in bed. *His.*
                        Each image projects
across this stranger's eyes, a boy who had the nerve
to look through his windshield, if only for a second, to invade
the calm, and the nerve to laugh at some inside joke.

Our hero's feet won't move, and the world presses against his chest,
three hundred invisible pounds standing on his rib cage
while the air whistles out.
                           He looks toward the glove box,
then looks away. To breathe again, he turns the key,
backs away, and turns the car toward home. In his rearview mirror
there's still the gathering of boys, white T-shirts blazing
in the neon light, voices breaking out in laughter.

A member of the group seems to yell while waving his arms.
The man in the driver's seat accelerates and almost hits
a frightened walker. "Punks," the man says at a level
only he can hear. He turns up the radio, which drowns the voices.
If he could hear, he'd know he was
driving into the dark with his headlights off.

Watching the Newtown Coverage While Cleaning a Weapon

Silence has blasted through the small screen,
and his careless quarry lies testament:
a plate lies face down in the basin;
a towel sags lifeless on a cold stove;
empty jeans have rolled from the sofa, legs gone limp.

Only the bodies on the muted screen move

and time moves, forward, backward.
Armored police park cars into a fortress and run,
scattering, toward a building whose white walls
burn themselves into foreign homes,

and a helicopter delivers
armchair detectives and surrogate shrinks
their god's-eye view.

The sky, two thousand miles away, constricts;

somewhere, maybe my neighbor's house,
a man loads shells by hand and speaks
to a blue-black barrel pointing skyward
against the wall. "I told you so," he says
to it,
          as if every face in every crowd
watched and waited. For what if the sun
prying through closed drapes threatened
to kill what grew in a dark, moist place,
to take what is secured by four walls,
what he grips with cold fingers?

Some days, it is what I have: to step past the door,
without barricades,
                              to say anything
that adds sound to a neighborhood gone mute,
to walk unarmed past windows, because
a constant vigil fed by fear
is not freedom.

These days, even the air refuses to move.
Grass blades slice and the clouds form a dome
overhead. A truck passes, Stars and Bars
filling the rear window; a face looks out with contempt.

With effort, I realize none of that is true.

Three doors down a child, playing alone,
retrieves his ball from a neighbor's yard.

He has not learned to be afraid of boundaries,
does not wonder what eyes lurk behind each window,

and his breath comes natural.

Somewhere, a man prays for an unseen hand
to strike down what he fears.
Another man prays for the words, to walk next door
and say "hello" to strangers.
I realize I am one of them,

and I do not know which,

but I am outside, wondering
if God has the volume turned up,
if he is tired of watching funerals,
if he is tired of both shooter and victim
screaming in his ear.

Or maybe, with the world on mute,
he sees only a solitary hand curl, which
looks clasped in prayer, which
looks like a fist shaking toward heaven, which
looks like a lover's hand holding another, which
looks like a mother's holding the smaller hand of a child, which
looks like a hand wrapping around a pistol grip
as if nothing else matters.

Cabin Dreams

...there can be more beauty and more deep wonder in the standings and
spacings of mute furnishings on a bare floor between the squaring bourns
of walls than in any music ever made...
—James Agee, Let Us Now Praise Famous Men

These photographs of tenant houses have become
less a view of other lives, more a black and white version
of my own. The doorless wooden frame beckons.

Here is where I hovered once outside an empty kitchen
where we'd stop before the steely basin that tilted without
falling from a loose and splintered shelf. Someone has filled
the bowl with cool water. Soon the daily dust will invade,
settling, floating like small drowned bodies on the surface.

This image freezes, dreamlike; a stillness belies the morning
sharecropper chores. A lone white towel hangs
from a lone nail, waiting to be darkened in the tar of men
who never come clean. Soon enough, dirty hands carrying
tobacco tar, tractor grease, some hay dust and mud
will plunge themselves beneath the surface, blend
with homemade soap.
                              After lunch and the half-satisfaction
of scraps, work will resume; the midday sun will begin its burn.
For now, edges hone themselves against an unseen sunrise.
An earthenware jar rests alone on a bare wooden cupboard,
and the scratch of hope's malnourished fingernail rasps
against handspun clay.
                              Dust has been swept from the table,
leaving only the unlit stare of a kerosene lamp.

Glass catches the sun in a fake ball of flame, and soot
hangs in its chimney walls of a stub of burned-out wick.
Only ash remains as evidence of late nights gathered
around this small but brilliant circle, fighting what terrors
make their presence known—a footstep crunching dry grass,
the exhalation of rough beasts, or the whistle, which is air
seeping through gaps in hastily built walls.

The mind wanders, coating the senses with fear.
Edges sharpen. My breath slows and the heart stills.
Edges become shapes of the familiar, and shadows retreat
from a window that must exist, slinking into corners.

Eyes dart over the photo of a life. I find myself filling
this cabin with names. Eyes notice a black, windowless
room. I want to let this alcove remain ambiguous,
but it fills the center of this dream; anxiety's night
forms a residue on this and future mornings.

Broken Clocks

The classroom clocks have stopped today;
electric pulses have gone silent.
A boy his age—he should have known.

"Disruption," says an adult in the room.
I mean, what boy his age would care
what makes the inner workings of time?

We thought it would be you; the man
in blue looks the boy from head to toe.
Split second decisions are what matter here.

The hour hands have turned to blades
while automatic fingers tap against veneer.
The adults in the room begin to wonder

where that ticking's coming from.
Wires and circuits change their function to match
the color of the hands that hold them.

And adults look with suspicion at the boy
who should have known, who's grown
still and silent, like a broken clock.

Corner of 2nd and State

The empty sea blue sky stretches; we're mute beneath it
save shouts from a nearby house. A siren wails.
A lady on the sidewalk crosses herself, muttering,
walking ahead. Two dogs inside a chain link fence
resume their barking when a boy rides past,
and though they never jump the fence the boy
quickens his pace. And on the road
a man in a pickup truck tailgates a foot behind
a compact car whose driver looks up, looks
worriedly, in her rearview. The duet continues,
she, gripping the steering wheel, the driver of the truck
gesturing, shouting words we cannot hear through glass.
They drive past the local church where a group
has gathered to pray over the sorry state of the world.
Rumor has it two men in town had dared fall in love,
and the lives of the righteous will never be the same.
In this moment, each looks angrily, worriedly,
toward the sky, which remains clear, blue and silent.

Astronomy

I find myself staring over the soft streetlight fire, focused
on the small pin lights in the air. I don't remember them being so small
but, then again, it seems like forever since I stepped outside and looked up.

Each sun exploded eons ago, leaving a message in braille, just out of reach.
Messages Brahe would live for, Galileo would die for; messages
al-Farghani decrypted before we became too stupid in our prejudice to honor.

All of us stare up beneath the same sky, pretending we discovered it.
I'm going to stare a while longer. Voices over the radio deny all of it:
the moon landing, the presence of other suns, even that the universe exists.
If the voices travel far enough, they may reach the stars,

who may decide it's not worth the effort, this burning
of one's own body for the sake of another.

A Culture of Fear

Only at night do we hear the voices of each creature—
desperate for the comfort of a vaguely familiar voice.
"Come, save us from our loneliness," we say as if crickets
sing for an audience or bullfrogs make guttural small talk.
The walls of our subdivision, on the edge of the country,
disappear with sunset. Now we have only the dirge
of distant tires, the percussion of closing doors,
this horror movie at the point all goes black
and we know the next sound will make us jump.
At night there is only space in the dark air. And we—
we're creating noise to save us from our imagination,
the mind that creates a world of sirens and footfalls
nearing our homes. A mind pacified by the hum of a round
stroking the inside of a chamber—its creations move us
to make orange halos in the dark, hoping the flash will
illuminate that invisible sound beyond our understanding.

Requiem for Miriam Carey

1.

Later, in a local diner, viewers will ask the question,
why a hygienist from up the seaboard would do it,
turn toward the White House in a black Infiniti,
then drive away, running over man and barricade.
"She don't look like a terrorist," someone will say.
Her picture, with a flawless smile, will enter
every living room for two nights before it is replaced
with the next tragedy.

2.

City cops and Secret Service will check their stories;
one will match the other. Her car will become a battering ram
crashing forward through the metal gates, then backward.
"We were afraid," someone will say—her speed
increased; her look became more menacing.

3.

The news will show her face twenty-four hours a day.
"She was a pretty thing," someone will say while dishing potatoes
onto a plate. Others will shake their heads, still eating.

4.

Rumors will fly as yellow tape is strung around her apartment.
Agents will carry her computer down the steps;
an expert on al Qaeda will give an opinion
on dental hygiene. In the capital, two women,
police officers, will carry a small girl with hair neatly tied,
a bright pink shirt, back turned. The cameras
will follow the little girl, drawing the question
out of viewers: "Who leaves someone this precious?"

5.

Time will pass; after dark, the word *drugs* will be said.
No one will say *prescription*. The *d* word will linger
on the lips of pundits and in the air. Her smile will appear
in the background, dissonant from the words
at the bottom of the screen. Tables will clear, leaving
late-night coffee drinkers and a lone waitress wiping tables
to glance upward at the screen. The words *postpartum
psychosis* will appear; the *d* word will become the *m* word,
and most Americans will be in bed.

6.

A wrong-turn theory will appear and be dismissed.
No one will think the innocent should panic
if they're innocent. By early morning, the breakfast
crowd will watch the story change from across the counter.
"I'd shoot her five times in the back, too,"
a voice will say, listing the reasons why. No one will look;
a lone fork will crash to the floor.

7.

Hours later, an expert on mental health will appear,
someone who can explain the feeling of walls closing in,
what happens when a person quits the medicine too soon,
how little panic has to do with reason. He will say this
while a last picture of that flawless smile hovers
in the background.
                    It seems a person possesses
both a flawless smile and terror, a mothering instinct
and a need for escape. Complexities will become apparent
in the middle of the day, after most have switched the channel.

Absalom

The world ends—choked in its own tangles.

He once thought peace might come
in life's final moments, piety's end drifting
to sleep in an old man's bed,
but dreams of peace diminish when
fathers turn away, leaving boys to do
the messy job an old man won't.

"Tamar," whose body became the end of peace,
is all he whispers from the air

while thinking of some infinitely patient one
hiding in a cave—waiting for what?
For a boy riding muleback on a rock-strewn path
to care about forgiveness of the old man's sins?

Sap runs through his scalp, and leaves circle
the young one's crown. Hair turns wooden.

The son understands the silent rage of trees
that can only watch would-be kings,
guided by invisible voices, cut them down.

Churning Through This Room

Electricity is churning through this hospital room,
finding its release in the chirps that mimic the pulse
of the living—the exhale, inhale of the ventilator
whose rubber lung fills and empties, keeping time
with the living. Voices carry from all directions.

My hands are wrist-deep in the circuitry of a machine,
one that should be infusing fluid into a vein
but has decided not to. I'm alone in the only spare
corner of the ward tonight, pulling a board
from its socket, cleaning the gold-toned contacts,
fitting everything back, possibly shaken a millimeter
off by some doctor feeling the weight of a man's life
and needing the manufactured world to work
as intended.
            Once my friend lay in a bed like this one,
a friend who told me books were a waste of time,
"They get nothing done." When he walked out of here,
he stopped in the gift store, pulled a Nat Geo from the shelf,
and slowly read it all the way home. At times he'd stop to tell
me what life crawled under the sands of Marrakech.

I snap the machine case back together and wonder
if he kept reading, if he kept breathing. An array of LEDs
light up. Everything flows again. The red electric bar
begins to move. An overhead voice, "Dr. Isaac to
room 317," means the world wants Mrs. Thompson a little
while longer. The steady beats of the living speak;
the ventilator sighs as it does its work. Then, together,
we exhale, making room for the next miraculous breath.

Upon Hearing "Hard Rock Returns to Prison from the Hospital for the Criminally Insane"

First time I heard this poem, I missed the meaning,
spent most of my ninth-grade day buzzing
from the fact my teacher just said "Shit" in class.
That's how we were those days, so well behaved.
There was a kid on the bus that everyone
called Stinky, who lived in a one-room tenement
shack. We'd make believe our seats were full
and stare away. Sometimes in church we'd
giggle. That's how it was those days.
So this poem about a man lobotomy-scarred,
docile as a farm animal, muscled arms
that could crush a man, hanging lifeless,
should have shown a larger world. But "shit"
was forbidden; that's how it was back then.
And our views of others came from dinner talk,
"others" and "those people," and "we won't ever go
on welfare." The adults would say it; we kids
would take it in. I thought we must have been
rich in other ways. Years later I learned the codes,
that men like Etheridge Knight had worked
to strip them from the language.

There were other words, more powerful ones,
but that profanity rattling in my brain was an act
of revolution. That's the way it needed to be back then.
But we didn't know, too busy indulging rumors
of welfare queens and busloads of out-of-towners
invading our polling booths. At dinner
someone spoke of dead men voting,
and I pictured the bodies rising from their graves
on Election Day. For years I'd keep an eye trained,
if we were driving in November, on each cemetery.
We'd laugh about coffee burns in McDonald's
and spotted owls. That's how it was back then
Codes sounded better than a face full of welts,
split purple lips, scars beneath each eyelid;
and they masked a smoldering rage
that matched a color code to every defect
of our souls.
        Codes were our lobotomy.

That's how it was back then. One day we rode
the bus along the riverfront and watched a man
limping in front of a ramshackle house.
A hand tapped my shoulder. Someone said,
"Look at that" and pointed toward the man.
In a minute I realized they were waiting on me,
the class clown, to tell the joke. "Shit," was all
I could muster, and while they in the seat behind me
laughed, the sun pushed like icepicks on my eyes.
That's how it felt then—the sweet, blessed pain.

Shrove Tuesday

I.

Winter's disappointment fades—a stack
of clearance-bin Christmas cards covers
the last bare corner of an unkempt house.
The life in images of snow-crested rooftops,
a honey gold fireplace, contrast the present
dark dry days, where even the sun at its
highest casts long shadows. If images dared
be honest, she would see green crabgrass
sprawling beneath broken stones,
the dull glow of low-hanging marble clouds.

II.

The owners of the house begin the process
of pulling excess from cabinet shelves.
A winter's worth of lard, bleached white flour,
some sugar—it all goes in the mixing bowl.
Even a grain mite, should it crawl through
the spider-webbed cracks in the walls, should
find nothing and pass right through. Tonight,
though, they'll celebrate tears, mourn laughter,
wake full, and begin the slow emptying out.

III.

Something of this feast seems funereal.
Green from hilltop cedar darkens, as do
the prickly cactus fans. Sun sinks; purple
shadows creep from what still dares to stand.
The old man and his wife are standing
in their yard to the last minute of sunlight.
She listens for the sound of wheels turning
onto gravel; he rests his arm on a jagged oak.
Dry. If a spark touched these hills, the fire
would eat it all, leaving only the limestone
bones emerging from the ground. He thinks
he's okay with that, wondering what,
if anything, was ever here to be had.

IV.

Dark falls and visitors drift in. Though people laugh,
it's become a dull cacophony, white noise.
Women tell stories in the living room; the men
segregate themselves onto a screened-in porch.
The owner watches through the windows.
He's smoking alone, crushing a fallen cherry
into the ground where cracks run like capillaries.
He looks at what electric light illuminates,
and in the haze he sees a spot of ash.

V.

There's heat lightning in the desert tonight.
Yes, in February. An electric charge pulls
each micro hair on his arms and neck up
to the heavens, a rebellion against gravity.
Just the air momentarily coming to life,
licking at the skin, and then—nothing.
"At least there's little to burn," he smirks
to only himself. He thinks of the words
that accompany fire—*consume, spread,
engulf.*
        "Bam!"
                Someone has yelled the word
for emphasis, shaking him from his thoughts.
The whole house fills with laughter
that crests for a second, then fades.

VI.

Back inside, the wife finds the husband,
repeats the joke—a funeral, a vicar, a missing body—
and they laugh, inappropriately, together,
lighter in the knowledge that everyone dies.

Full belly, empty belly, watered or wilted in the sun.

Soon the crowd thins, bread and pastries vanish,
and then it's just the two of them, silently
washing plates, talking through the random look

until, just before turning in, they hear it:
a first drop of rain, much like a pulse of blood
against the onionskin of an eardrum beginning
to quicken—a next drop, and a next—
until the ground comes alive, with...

(too late, he places his hand over his lips).
                                        It's the sound
of jazz brushes rolling across a snare. For one last
moment before bedtime, he steps out beneath the clouds,
catches water in his palms. And while he knows
this has nothing to do with feast or fast, it can't hurt,
in this moment in the desert, to imagine it does.

Aubade: Monk's Pond

Before the cidered glow creates
the world again, two stumble.

Measured steps of blind petitioners
demand proof and night's fingers
discover, in turns, the velvet of loam,
cuts from sycamore root and briar,

or waking,
                    marvel how a warm sachet
of flesh covers a valley of bone.

The world ends on a cold glass pane.

"Stop," she says, "I haven't been born."

Murmurings of wild voices echo
and unseen feet create ripples,
drumming slowly beneath the surface.
Light cuts its hue on the whetstone of clouds,
setting water ablaze,
                              severs
the tops of trees from the sky
that weeps at his loss.

In the tears, twin branches plumb downward
and winged arbiters glide on the surface between.

Small Gods

Orion hangs his belt over the western woods.
He has turned in for the night, and the small gods
begin to emerge from their hiding spaces.
Dogs have begun their call and response;
a raccoon's ringed tail slips under the fence.
Even the small boulder, after a day of gathering
the sun—for a few hours, abundance—
radiates outward. And on its flat surface,
scorpion rests, eight legs clinging, in the vanishing
light of a still night, to what remains.

Rising in Flyover Country

The hum over asphalt in a fiberglass bubble
rides synthetic black before meeting
its end on the grated rumble
of cattle crossings.

Or is it

the barely perceptible rawhide and horns
shifting at night, outside the reach
of headlight beams? This is no bullet
train through flyover country.

The road changes through hairpin turns,
switchbacks, hills that floated as mirage,

fifty miles back, in the flatlands. A rickety
white bridge passes one car at a time.

Outside the light,

longhorn, elk and buffalo have been known
to lie on the still-warm pavement, in the dark;
inconvenient, they rest over hillcrests
where speeding visitors careen
into an avalanche of rock and screams.

And an unfinished life
occupies the last thoughts,
because no one thought a journey,
riding the bubble, required a speech.

The wise lower windows,
take a foot off the accelerator,
and notice the aroma of tall prairie grasses,
redbud, magnolia, wild animal scat.

Country music twangs from across the bridge,
and for once it comforts.

The night has a spine of blacktop
down the middle,
connected by stone ribs
to the unseen
                    where the wild things roam.

Acknowledgments

Grateful acknowledgment is given to the following publications in which these poems appeared, some in earlier versions.

Appalachian Heritage: "Cadiz," "Three Battles in the Hill Country,"
     "Cave Country," "One Night in Early Spring"
The Good Men Project: "Orange," "Shanty Hollow," "Shooting Silhouettes,"
     "Old War Movies and the News," "Mapmaking," "The Fearmongers,"
     "The Foyer of a Soldier's House," "A Culture of Fear"
Grey Sparrow Journal: "Circular Logic"
The Lookout: "Our House Is Alarmed," "Villanelle for Charleston"
O-Dark Thirty: "Retreat"
Poets and War: "Blackhawk Crash," "Overwatch"
Red River Review: "Broken Clocks"
The Sewanee Review: "The Mortar's Whistle," "Transubstantiation"
Snow Jewel: "Tolling"
Still: The Journal: "Lime," "Nocturne"
War, Literature and the Arts: "Negative Space"
The Windhover: "Compline"
Zetetic: A Record of Unusual Inquiry: "Come Winter"

Cover artwork, photo of cave entrance by Artur Roman; author photo by Allyson Chandler; cover and interior book design by Diane Kistner; ITC Highlander text and titling

About FutureCycle Press

FutureCycle Press is dedicated to publishing lasting English-language poetry books, chapbooks, and anthologies in both print-on-demand and Kindle ebook formats. Founded in 2007 by long-time independent editor/publishers and partners Diane Kistner and Robert S. King, the press incorporated as a nonprofit in 2012. A number of our editors are distinguished poets and writers in their own right, and we have been actively involved in the small press movement going back to the early seventies.

The FutureCycle Poetry Book Prize and honorarium is awarded annually for the best full-length volume of poetry we publish in a calendar year. Introduced in 2013, our Good Works projects are anthologies devoted to issues of universal significance, with all proceeds donated to a related worthy cause. Our Selected Poems series highlights contemporary poets with a substantial body of work to their credit; with this series we strive to resurrect work that has had limited distribution and is now out of print.

We are dedicated to giving all of the authors we publish the care their work deserves, making our catalog of titles the most diverse and distinguished it can be, and paying forward any earnings to fund more great books.

We've learned a few things about independent publishing over the years. We've also evolved a unique, resilient publishing model that allows us to focus mainly on vetting and preserving for posterity poetry collections of exceptional quality without becoming overwhelmed with bookkeeping and mailing, fundraising activities, or taxing editorial and production "bubbles." To find out more about what we are doing, come see us at www.futurecycle.org.

The FutureCycle Poetry Book Prize

All full-length volumes of poetry published by FutureCycle Press in a given calendar year are considered for the annual FutureCycle Poetry Book Prize. This allows us to consider each submission on its own merits, outside of the context of a contest. Too, the judges see the finished book, which will have benefitted from the beautiful book design and strong editorial gloss we are famous for.

The book ranked the best in judging is announced as the prize-winner in the subsequent year. There is no fixed monetary award; instead, the winning poet receives an honorarium of 20% of the total net royalties from all poetry books and chapbooks the press sold online in the year the winning book was published. The winner is also accorded the honor of being on the panel of judges for the next year's competition; all judges receive copies of all contending books to keep for their personal library.

www.ingramcontent.com/pod-product-compliance
Lightning Source LLC
Chambersburg PA
CBHW070002100426
42741CB00012B/3101